Free Confinement

Survival in Europe 1941 - 45

Eva Hirschenstein Appelbaum

Table of Contents

Introduction

This memoir about my family's experience during WWII has been developing for many years. I started making notes in the 1970s on any piece of paper available when a certain recollection came to me. I thought the story was worth telling for the following reasons: first, because my parents and I managed to escape the death camps – through repeated strokes of luck and with the help of many people, in particular, the officers and the soldiers of the Italian Army; second, to relate how a young child experienced these harrowing events, often finding more adventure than fear; and third, to preserve these memories for my children and my grandchildren.

Unfortunately by the time I started writing this narrative and realized how sketchy some of my memories were, my parents had both died. I regret that I don't know the names of the private individuals who put their safety in jeopardy for us. On the other hand, the names of General Mario Roatta, Commander of the Italian 2nd Army in Yugoslavia and General Mario Robotti, who later replaced him, are a matter of historical record. And there were many others - officers, soldiers, diplomats in Rome, including Mussolini's Foreign Minister, Count Galeazzo Ciano - who took the plight of Croatian Jews, of whom I was one, to heart. To them and to my family I dedicate this writing.

Zagreb, Yugoslavia, 1941

It was Easter morning. Mother and father exchanged worried glances over breakfast as they read the daily papers bearing large headlines printed in red. Not yet seven, I could tell that this was no ordinary Sunday.
Later that day from the window of my room I saw German tanks roll up our street lined with tall chestnut trees. On other occasions I had watched religious processions with children dressed as angels and marching bands making their way up that same street. Memories of my early childhood in Zagreb exist as fragments but from that day on, as the regular rhythm of my daily life was disrupted, I recorded events in a more or less sequential order.

When Hitler invaded Yugoslavia in 1941 he bombed the city of Belgrade mercilessly and easily overcame the Serbian forces that attempted resistance.
There was no resistance in Croatia and its capital, Zagreb, as the Croats had long fought for an independent state and were promised one by Hitler. Ante Pavelic, the leader of the Ustase, the fascist Croatian movement, installed himself as ruler of Croatia without opposition from Hitler or Mussolini.
Pavelic had gained notoriety when he organized the assassination of King Alexander of Yugoslavia and the French Minister Louis Barthouin who were meeting in Marseille in November 1934. As soon as Pavelic

came to power, in 1941, he enacted the Racial Laws of his German Allies and with the help of the Ustase, proceeded to enforce them

My parents were not rich, but we lived in a two-bedroom apartment in a middle-class neighborhood. My room, the nursery, was sunny with large windows and cream-colored furniture. I used to sit on the floor and busy myself for hours constructing objects out of old thread spools and other items that were no longer of any use in the adult world. The dining room had a table of dark wood surrounded by Empire-style chairs upholstered in green and beige checks. From that table, when I was three or four, I once sent my dish of noodles with one clean sweep of my little hand crashing to the floor. I wound up in bed without dinner.

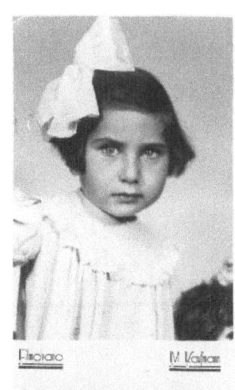

Eva age four

Both my parents worked. Father traveled for Shell Oil Company; mother was a secretary in a large lumber firm called Nasicka. (Yugoslavia is rich in forests, and timber is one of its main exports.) My mother's family lived in Hungary; her father was the caretaker of an estate which belonged to an Esterhazy, one of the Hungarian nobility. Mother was the oldest of seven siblings whom she helped to raise; when she was in her early twenties she was sent to Trieste to live with an aunt and to study to become a secretary. After finishing school she was expected to support herself and went to find work in Zagreb. In the 1920s, Zagreb was the second largest city in the new Kingdom of

Olga, my Mother

Yugoslavia, established out of several Balkan states previously part of the Austro-Hungarian Empire, by the victorious allies of World War I. Zagreb, the capital of Croatia, where artists, writers, and architects convened, had growing industries and business flourished.

My father's parents lived in the Croatian province of Bjelovar, then part of Austro-Hungary, where my grandfather was State Attorney. When my grandfather died of pneumonia on July 22, 1899, at age 38, his wife was pregnant with their second child. My father was born on January 3, 1900 and was given his father's name, Leopold. Soon after his birth my

Leo, my Father

grandmother moved back to her native Vienna with my father and her first child, my Uncle Rudy. There she opened a coffeehouse and met and married a Mr. Feric who was a gambler and eventually lost her business.

My dad did not get along with his stepfather. As a teenager, wanting to get out of the house at any cost, he tried to join the Merchant Marine but was rejected; they told him it was because he had a weak left eye, although he was convinced it was because he was Jewish. At the age of 17, he lied about his age, enlisted in the Austrian army and went to fight in World War I on the Italian front. He was taken prisoner by the Italians who in that war were allied with the French, the British, and the United States. While in prison in Verona – the beautiful city renowned for its unhappy lovers Romeo and Juliet – he contracted typhoid fever and almost died. My father told me how the nuns, who usually nursed hospital patients in those days, stood around his bed where he lay in a semi-coma, in their white winged bonnets, rosaries in hand murmuring the prayers for the dying. Something in his nature rebelled; he was not going to die, he would fight the sickness and live. He started on a slow but steady recovery. Released at the end of the war, he returned to a Vienna now defeated and in dismal economic condition. At first, father tried to help his family, which now included little Stefan his half -brother ten years his junior. He stood on lines to get milk and bread, and tried in vane to find any kind of work

Father eventually decided to leave Vienna and seek work elsewhere. Again, Yugoslavia and in particularl Zagreb was a natural destination.

There he met my mother and they married in 1927. My parents saved money and waited to be financially comfortable before having their first and only child, a daughter born seven years into their marriage.

Until age three or four, I had a nurse who doubled as a housekeeper. She came from the country nearby, a big, easygoing woman, whom my parents referred to as *debela Jelka*, "fat Jelka". As a toddler I tagged along as she attended to her household chores, including following her to the basement where she did the laundry by rubbing it on an old-fashioned washboard then sterilizing it in boiling water. I had a toy washboard on which I could wash my doll's cloths alongside Jelka. (I still remember the steamy, soapy odor that pervaded the basement.) Jelka took me along when she went shopping to the outdoor market where the peasants brought their produce from the countryside. One woman from whom Jelka bought sweet butter would cut a chunk of it with her special tool (a string stretched at the end of a bow), and hand it to me to eat. It tasted sweet, rich and delicious.

When I was born my parents lived at Ilica 143, a long street with many stores including an electrical supply shop on the ground floor of our building and a very large toy store further down the road where, my mother recalled, I would always announce that I wanted something. I was particularly fond of multicolored glass marbles that came in little net-like bags with a string closure. New York's F.A.O. Schwarz, which I often visited when my children were little, in the 60s and 70s, reminded me of that toy store.

My father had a beige Ford assigned to him by Shell Oil. Its license plate was 1167, easy to remember because in Serbo-Croatian the numbers one and seven rhyme. Despite spending many working days on the road he liked taking mother and me on weekend outings into the beautiful countryside surrounding Zagreb. I used to sit in the back seat, my nose glued to the window taking in all the sights. One of my favorite memories is of crossing a river on a raft inside the car. Tall reeds grew at the water's edge and beautiful trees could be seen along the embankment on the other side.

A small enameled metal plate decorated in red and orange, and silver-plated child-sized utensils always came along to feed me at inns and picnics when we stopped for lunch.I still have the spoon in my kitchen drawer in New York. On the Sava River, which runs on the outskirts of Zagreb and beyond, were establishments where one could bathe.

It was there that my father first taught me how to swim with an inflatable red rubber doughnut, sometimes carrying me on his back. He was of athletic build and as a young man in Austria, he used to climb mountains and pretend he knew the height of all the peaks. When, on a long walk, I complained "my little legs hurt," he would hoist me on his shoulders and carry me. I adored my father, but at the same time, I was afraid of him; he could get cross if I spilled or broke something, as children often do.

When we did not leave the city, on special occasions, I was taken to a beautiful hotel called the Esplanade for cake and hot chocolate. We were served on a large terrace overlooking a square planted with trees and flowers.

Many years later my husband and I spent a night at that hotel when we took a detour to Zagreb during a summer vacation on the Adriatic coast. It was 1986, before the fall of Communism and the subsequent breakup of Yugoslavia.

It was my only trip back. The hotel did not disappoint my memory even if it was a little seedy and had very few guests. The hotel staff whom I spoke with in Croatian, a language I still speak fairly well, could not have been more helpful, including getting tickets for us for the ballet "Swan Lake" being performed that evening at the Zagreb National Theater. I had seen "Swan Lake" there almost 50 years before and I had not forgotten the dancing, the costumes, the stage and the balconies in red and gold.

Mother was a good-looking woman who dressed elegantly. My favorite was a silk summer dress with short sleeves. It was black, printed with small white blossoms and tiny green leaves. She went to the hairdresser every week and once when she took me along they used a curling iron to turn my very straight hair into curls *a la* Shirley Temple. Having seen one or two of her films, I was in seventh heaven, shaking my head in front of the mirror, imagining I now looked like her.

My parents were not religious, despite the fact that my father's great-grandfather was a rabbi. Still, we used to go to Temple for the High Holidays. The Zagreb Synagogue was quite beautiful, decorated in blue and gold; it was destroyed in 1941 by the Ustasa regime.

There were also trips to Hungary when mother took me along to visit her parents and her sisters and brothers. On one of those trips we had an overnight stay in Budapest in a hotel where the room overlooked the Danube River and tall windows were framed by beautiful curtains.

In the double bed where I was left alone for an afternoon nap I fantasized I was a princess. I remember the huge Budapest railway station where we waited, sitting on the round ottoman-like chairs upholstered in deep red leather,
 for the train that would take us to the small town where my grandparents lived.

When I was four or five, Jelka left. Maria, a German governess, took care of me and taught me German, which I can still speak well enough to get by in a pinch. German was the language of the Zagreb intellectuals; the city was called the little Vienna of the East during the Austro-Hungarian Empire.

Maria was tall, slim and serious, with a braided blond tress wound around her head. She took me to the park, but mother later said, she never let me stray too far from her side or play with other children lest I get dirty.

Perhaps that is why I learned to amuse myself alone, most of the time playing house next to the roots of large oaks and plane trees that graced Zagreb's parks, or collecting the colorful leaves that covered the ground in autumn. If you look through my books these days you can still find a maple or birch leaf from Central Park, drying between the pages.

I did have occasional playmates. My favorite was my cousin Mladen, a very distant cousin, an only child like myself, very blond, about my age. I visited him on weekends with my mother and father. His parents had a small private home in the suburbs and in their yard we played doctor and patient and since he took the lead in any game, I was always the patient. I used to say I would marry him when we grew up. In the late 1970s I visited him, his wife and children in Haifa, Israel, only this time I was the physician.

There is one other friend I had in Zagreb before the war. His name was Dancek, the only child of a well-to-do physician. His family lived in a beautiful apartment with a large brick stove covered in reddish-brown majolica tiles. He had a governess who was quite creative and taught us how to make flowers with colorful crepe and tissue paper.

Dancek was ill; he spent most of the time sitting in a chair. He and his parents saved themselves by immigrating to Argentina. After the war I found out details of his illness and the rest of his tragic history from my parents and from his uncle, Mr. Zvjezdic. He was my father's best friend, who like us had escaped from Zagreb and now lived in Rome. Dancek had contracted TB of the hip as a young child. Despite numerous treatments and surgeries, a limp and chronic pain persisted into his adulthood. In his thirties, by then a physician himself, he took his own life.

There was an unhappy attempt to send me to school; I can still see myself standing, all alone, during recess in a corner of the large schoolyard that was surrounded by a tall wall. I am not sure if it was because I was too shy or because the other children ignored me since the racial laws prohibited Gentiles from associating with Jews.

After the German troops entered Zagreb, Maria started meeting German soldiers in the park and spending much time talking with them while holding me tight by the hand at her side. She must have been indoctrinating me well about her *fuehrer*, since one day I dressed in my white shirt and little red bathing suit pretending I was Hitler, a memory I would love to erase. Eventually, she suggested to my mother that it would be a good idea if she took me with her to Germany. I remember the two women standing in the room arguing. Mother later recounted how at some point Maria blurted out, "Anyway I am not supposed to work for Jews." Mother promptly told her to get out of the house and I don't think I was sorry to see Maria go. In retrospect it is possible that she had heard from her soldier friends what our fate was to be and wanted at least to save the child she had grown fond of.

My next babysitter was *Tante* (Aunt) Rosenberg who started teaching me English (father had often toyed with the idea of emigrating to the US). She wasn't my aunt and perhaps her name was Rosen-something else, I no longer remember, but I do remember she was a loving older woman who treated me like a small adult, a rare treat in those days when children were expected to be seen but not heard. One day she was gone. My parents later told me she had been deported.

After Tante Rosenberg left, my parents sent me for a few days to my grandmother and my step-grandfather, who lived in a small apartment in one of the new houses built on the outskirts of Zagreb.

After WWI my grandmother, Mr. Feric, and Uncle Rudy had remained in Vienna where Uncle Rudy worked for a large insurance company. In 1938 Hitler marched into Austria welcomed by the population, and annexed Austria to greater Germany, the *Anschluss,* as it was called. Persecution of Jews followed rapidly, leading to loss of jobs, confinement to ghettoes and then removal to death camps, euphemistically referred to as: "resettlement to the East".

Thinking that they would be safer in Yugoslavia, Dad brought the three members of his family to Zagreb where Uncle Rudy was able to find work with the same insurance company he had worked for in Vienna. (Uncle Stefan, my father's half-brother, had left Austria earlier and by then was living safely in Ireland.)

I liked being at my grandmother's. I can still visualize the stocky woman moving about in her small kitchen, with her grey hair tied in a tight knot in the back of her neck. She had very dark eyes, like my father's and Uncle Rudy's, inherited from her grandmother who was a Sephardic Jew, a descendant of the Jews of Spain expelled by Ferdinand and Isabella in 1492.

Behind the apartment building, there was a railroad yard with big heaps of coal. I soon found a little friend, a boy my age, who informed me that he was not supposed to play with me because I was Jewish, but he was not prepared to obey the interdiction. We used to buy a few chewy, sour candies from the corner grocery and play war climbing the mountain of coal. I came back to the apartment black like a chimney sweep. My grandmother washed me and changed me without a harsh word. At home I was expected to keep clean and dainty. My step-grandfather took me for long walks in the neighborhood and bought me raspberries that were sold for a few pennies in small paper cones. Here at the periphery of the city there were large building sites left abandoned because of the war. The holes in the ground where large cranes stood idle fascinated me. You can still catch me peeping between the slots of fences wherever a skyscraper is coming up in Manhattan.

My grandmother, Mr. Feric, and Uncle Rudy, were killed in Jasenovac, unable or unwilling to leave. Uncle Rudy told father that his employers had promised to protect him and he believed them.

Incremental enactment of racial laws and persecution of Jews continued. Jews were ordered to wear, clearly visible on their outer clothing, a yellow patch with the Star of David printed in black. I thought there was a photo

Uncle Rudy

of me wearing the yellow patch on my spring coat but as I have been unable to find it, I am beginning to wonder if what I remembered was actually my image reflected in the mirror. The Ustase, Pavelic's militia, who were later described as being not only equal to the German SS, but even more merciless, raided Jewish homes in Zagreb, picked up entire families and transferred them to camps or executed them on the spot. One couple living in a beautiful private stone house, further up on our tree-lined street, jumped to their death when the Ustase came to pick them up.

The camp near Zagreb called Jasenovac is infamous for the number of Serbs, Gypsies, and Jews who were killed there. One of my parents' friends, Mr. Donner, a well-to-do butcher with whom mother had played tennis since her youth, was taken to Jasenovac and narrowly escaped death when his wife, with a well-placed bribe, was able to obtain his release.

Of the estimated 82,000 Jews living in Yugoslavia before the war, approximately 15,000 survived.

Our last address in Zagreb was *Amruseva 7*, as father reported to the Authorities on May 14, 1941. I have a photo of the entrance to the building that my daughter Irene took on a trip to Yugoslavia in the 80's. Jews were allocated a limited amount of living space per person so families consolidated to comply. We moved in with the Milhofers whose apartment, not far from ours, was larger than the one we lived in. Their familial nucleus mirrored ours: a mother, a father, and a little girl my age, my friend Ruth or *Rutica* in Croatian. Her mother and mine both worked for *Nasicka* the wood export company. We played together every day, only dimly aware of the circumstances that had brought us together. We chatted with each other from windows of opposing bathrooms while brushing our teeth, getting ready for bedtime. One day Ruth decided to give me a haircut, which I suspect was not a masterpiece. I was surprised at the relatively mild reaction from parents on both sides.

Occasionally I would visit another little girl who lived nearby. To get there I had to cross the street and I was quite proud that I was allowed to go alone. Clearly the grown-ups were not behaving as expected, yet I don't believe I was ever told anything about what was going on around us nor did it occur to me to ask. Children were not encouraged to ask questions and as far as possible, my parents always shielded me from anything unpleasant.

One day Ruth and her parents left the apartment in an attempt to flee to safety. Ruth's father was a pharmacist and professionals were among the first to get picked up by the Ustase. Many years later, after the war, I had occasion to visit Ruth's parents in Haifa, Israel where they had resettled. I never saw Ruth who lived in a different city. She was one of a group of children who, early in the war, were allowed to leave for Israel. Ruth spent the war years there away from her parents. The Milhofers told me she had suffered from the long separation.

After the Milhofers left we were alone in the apartment. Mother and father had been laid off. Even before she was fired, mother recalled later, colleagues with whom she had shared goulash for lunch a week before, looked the other way when they passed her in the hallway. Yet there were decent people as well, as we would find out during our long road to safety. While searching through my parents' documents, I discovered a letter to the authorities from the director of Nasicka, stating that mother was a valued employee and should be allowed to continue working undisturbed. The letter was dated July 1941. Shell Oil Company fired my father in June of that year.

Late one afternoon the doorbell rang. Father went to open the door. I was in the hallway next to my red tricycle and saw two men in fedoras and trench coats standing right outside our apartment. "We are looking for Dr. Milhofer," one of them said. My father told them he and his family had left the day before and, no, he did not know where they were.

"Well in that case we want you to come instead of him. Report to the police with your wife and child, tomorrow morning."

Tomorrow morning? Were they giving us a break? Did they have some decency left? Was it the sight of the child, the tricycle? Had they taken us away with them or had we complied with the order the following day, we would have been removed to the death camp of Jasenovac outside Zagreb, killed there or dispatched by trains to Auschwitz. We were given a reprieve and this was the first of many occasions where luck along with the help of courageous people helped us survive.

We left the apartment the same night with whatever could be packed into two suitcases. I remember my parents arguing about what to take and what to leave. My doll Linda (she was named after my Hungarian Uncle Lajosh's horse) with her dark pageboy hair and eyes that closed when you put her head down, did not make it; my teddy bear, which accompanied me in the car on weekend trips, did, as did some of the clothes that would have to do for quite a few years to come. These two old suitcases and my toy teddy bear were with us throughout the war, and while the former are long gone, the bear is now perched high on an old bookcase, his glass eyes lost, his fur worn but his head still moves when you wag his tail. Mother had undone one of the animal's paws, hidden money inside and sewn it closed again. More cash was hidden in her girdle. When we moved in with the Milhofers, my parents left a few of their belongings with Catholic friends who kept them safe and returned them after the war. A beautiful small Persian rug is now owned by one of my daughters.

After we left the apartment, we spent the night at a relative's house in a different part of town. The small dining room was crowded with people who hoped to catch a train to safety in the morning. What I remember of that night are the tall windows covered with blue paper and tape in observance of the blackout. I must have fallen asleep on a couch while my eyes wandered over the delicate objects in a china closet set against the opposite wall.

Running and Hiding

The next morning we boarded the train at the station. It was the same train that just a few years before had taken us to the seaside resort where we spent our summer vacations. Soon we were in a compartment. Father placed the suitcases on the rack, then sat next to my mother on the seat opposite me. Next to me sat a small Jewish woman, in her forties, wearing a white blouse with black polka dots. She soon engaged me in conversation, again, speaking to me as if I were a little adult. I never learned the woman's name or her fate, since years later I was only able to call her "the woman in the polka dot blouse" and my parents were not sure who she was. In a similar fashion, during that time of uncertainty, men, women and children appeared and disappeared with many questions unanswered.

The train left the station and tense faces relaxed a little. We had a permit to travel to the coast and back. The permit was dated July 15, 1941 and we were supposed to return by July 31st.

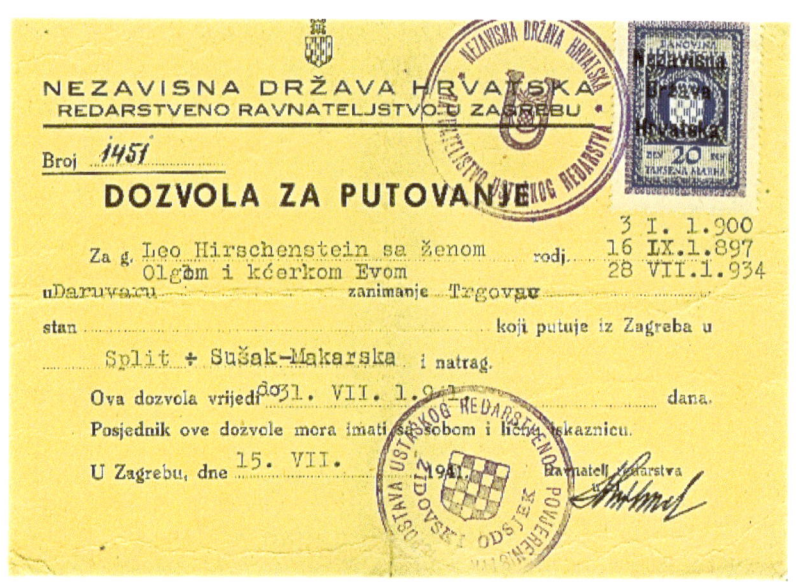

Permit to Travel

The plan was to seek protection in Italian occupied Territory and never return.

When the Germans invaded Yugoslavia in April 1941, Mussolini's forces rushed to occupy part of Yugoslavia, so the country was now divided into a German zone and an Italian zone – the latter comprised half of Croatia, and all of Dalmatia and Montenegro. In the summer of 1941, appalled by the brutal massacres occurring in the German zone at the hands of the Ustase, the Italian Army, under the command of General Vittorio Ambrosio, offered safe haven in the Italian zone to the Jews of Croatia who were lucky enough to escape. This was done without prior approval from Rome and Mussolini.

Perhaps an hour outside Zagreb the train stopped. It was a small station called Plase, one of those stations you frequently see along the European rail system where only a signpost with the name of the town and a platform remind the train to stop. Men with rifles moved rapidly through the corridor shouting: "All Jews off the train!" Although our passports did not indicate our religion, Jewish surnames were easy to recognize. We got off.

We remained there on the platform, a group of fifteen to thirty people with our luggage, while the train in front of us was given the signal to leave. The men with the rifles marched us to a school in the nearby village, a low building with woods at the far end suggesting we were at the edge of town. From my seven-year-old perspective the setting did not look very different from the country inns where we stopped for lunch or dinner on our weekend trips before the war.

Inside the building we were directed to a classroom where a man of average build, about forty, whom his comrades called *Bubanj* ("Drum" in Croatian), ordered us to place our suitcases on the desks and open them. He then went from one to the next and proceeded to take whatever pleased him. He took mother's silk stockings and, among other items, her favorite lizard shoes. She never forgave him for the shoes. This was evident every time she told and retold the story in the immediate postwar period as friends shared their stories of escape and survival. After plundering everyone's belongings, Bubanj let us go. We ran through the woods and reached a nearby lakeshore where a boatman took us to the other side. My guess is he got paid handsomely for his service. Warning shots rang through the air as the boat left the shore.

On the other side of the lake we had to climb a steep hill. There was no trail. We had to make our way between rocks and low vegetation. I was carrying a backpack. I slipped on the uncertain terrain and fell without hurting myself. The backpack hit the ground with the crackling sound of a thermos breaking. My father turned around. I looked up scared, expecting to be scolded. "Are you all right? Did you hurt yourself?" He was not worried about the broken thermos. When we reached the top of the hill my family separated from the group. From then on, the three of us were alone. We walked to a village with a few scattered peasant homes. In one of these a middle-aged couple dressed in black gave us refuge. They shared with us their simple food and let us sleep in their bedroom. There was a large bed in the middle of the room. It was made of dark wood, very plain, unadorned. On the opposite side was a washstand and on it was a beautiful ceramic basin and a pitcher full of water. That was how we washed up. We dried ourselves with the white towel hanging on the side of the washstand. Everything in that house was simple and immaculate and with that simplicity I had a warm feeling of safety that I would not have for several years to come.

I now find it strange that I have a recollection of how I felt on that occasion because most of the time I only registered events. Of course we were not really safe, nor were the kind people who had opened their house to us. It was Ustase territory. We had to move on; we made our way down to the coast of Dalmatia occupied by the Italian forces. Years later father gave to the Italian authorities July 1941 as our date of entry into Italy.

Susak

We arrived in Susak. The city lies on one side of a river and is in Yugoslavia, while on the other side, the city of *Rijeka* or *Fiume*, ("River" in Croatian and Italian, respectively) had been annexed to Italy in 1924. The Italian forces, allied with Hitler, were on both sides, but in the occupied territory they would soon come under mounting pressure to surrender the Croatian Jews back to the German zone where the Germans, with eager help from the Ustase, were implementing their plan to rid Europe of the Jewish people. Again we found loving, courageous people who offered their home as a safe haven.

The large house was reached by descending a narrow path from the main road. Behind the house was an orchard where vegetables grew in neat rows and where I was to spend many hours playing by myself. The house belonged to a mother and daughter team; the men were away fighting in the war. We were given a bedroom upstairs. We remained in that house for five or six months. My parents, especially my father who had very distinctive Semitic features, rarely left the house. On the other hand, I was sometimes allowed to go shopping with the landlady's daughter who, if asked, was prepared to tell the authorities I was her niece. Once she took me to Fiume across the river and there we visited a street fair where the landlady's daughter bought me a tiny wire devil with a big red tongue, a long tail and a pitchfork in his hand. This early experience later inspired me to make little wire creatures elaborately dressed in costumes made of felt, often given as gifts to family and friends. I kept a few of them as souvenirs. Downstairs was a large living room with a couch. The landlady had a black dachshund with brown paws. The dog and I soon became good friends; in the evening I would curl up on the couch next to him and pretended to play Rummy with him.

One day my mother and I went to a lawyer's office to see if he could obtain papers for the two of us to go to Hungary. Father was not going to join us. My maternal grandmother and my mother's two sisters and three brothers still lived there. My grandfather had died of cancer before the war.

Hungary was governed by Admiral Miklos Horthy. He was the Hungarian Regent who had signed a pact with Hitler in April 1941, which stated that he would help with the invasion of Greece in exchange for autonomy. Until 1943 he was able to protect the Hungarian Jews from deportation. In October 1943 Horthy was seized by the Germans, irritated by his lack of cooperation in implementing the Final Solution. He was removed and replaced by a German government. Adolph Eichmann saw personally to the deportation of Jews from Hungary, which intensified in 1944 as the Russian Army approached Hungary.

I distinctly recall the slightly heavy-set, balding man sitting behind an imposing desk who tried to be friendly to the little girl and asked me if I knew how many steps a sparrow takes a year, and while I was trying to guess, "None" he said, "a sparrow takes no steps, it jumps."

The lawyer was unable to obtain the necessary papers so we stayed with father in Susak. Had my mother and I succeeded in reaching Hungary we would have been on one of the late transports that in 1944 took hundreds of thousands of Hungarian Jews, including my grandmother and my Aunt Irena, to Auschwitz where most went straight to the gas chambers. Aunt Paula, the youngest of mother's sisters, was married to a Catholic engineer who took his wife and three children out of Hungary before the German onslaught. Two of my uncles, Jeno and Istvan died in Hungarian labor camps in1942. My mother was notified of these events in writing in October of 1945. I saw her standing in the room reading the letter and crying. Her other brother, Lajos, his young wife, and infant child were shot without ever leaving Hungary.

But I must go on with my story. I am still in Susak playing in the orchard behind our house, eating the little green peppers that grew on the vine and talking to "Red" the big cat that sunned itself in the yard. One day I found a gas mask hidden under the vegetables, perhaps left there by a soldier or stolen from the invading army and hidden by someone who forgot or was unable to retrieve it. When I took the mask into the house and showed it to my parents they were quite dismayed and asked me to take it right back to where I found it.

From my parents, I heard that a little friend of mine from Zagreb, whose name was Tommy, was also in Susak with his parents. I found out where he lived and decided to go visiting. Getting there was not a problem and spending time with my playmate was fun, but I was not home by curfew and my parents were extremely worried. I did get scolded that time. What I did not realize until much later is that had I been picked up by the patrol I could have led them to the house where we were hiding, endangering the whole family and our benefactors. Tommy and his parents made it safely to Italy where we met again in 1943.

Not all the Italian Authorities were willing to cooperate with the Army's decision to protect us. Perhaps tipped off by someone, or knowing all along where we were, one day the Italian police showed up at the house. They arrested father and put him on a train back to Yugoslavia where he was to be surrendered to the Ustase. Father knew that the Ustase would kill him. As he had been placed in an open cattle car, when the train slowed down in the countryside, he jumped off and, running through fields and hiding, made it back to Susak. Reared by Hollywood films and armed with a strong visual imagination, I can see the freight car, my father at the edge of the opening, jumping out into the tall grasses and running.

After that, father never left the room. He grew a moustache, thinking: "This way the Italian Police won't recognize me." He stayed in his pajamas all day and when they came again to look for him they found him in bed claiming he was ill. They took mother instead. My mother, who many years after the war would wear her Helena Rubinstein makeup and gold necklace to go to the neighborhood shopping center in Queens where the Italian merchants called her *La Contessa,* spent two or three nights in jail sharing a cell with common criminals and prostitutes. We saw her again when we were taken to a gathering place with other Croatian Jews also hiding in Susak. She was disheveled, looked older, and out of place with her seal-collared coat.

But we did not have to hide any more! Refusing to bow to continued German pressure, the Italians decided to move us further south, on the Dalmatian coast and place us in what was called: "free confinement".

Selce: Free Confinement

The small town we were assigned to was called
Selce. We were allowed to move around freely within
the town's confines with the requirement to obtain a
special permit from the police if we wanted to visit a
nearby town for the day. The Italian soldiers were
visible everywhere. In the evenings they used to sit in
front of their quarters and play *"morra"*, a numbers
game where two individuals shout quickly a number
from one to ten, simultaneously extending one to five
fingers of one hand. If a player shouted the total
number of fingers extended, he got points. At the
time it all looked very mysterious.

We lived in a small house with a tiny garden in the
back, not far from the seawall. The house had an attic
where corn flour was stored. It was a good hiding
place for a youngster wanting privacy. Mother made
good use of the corn flour, the only kind available at
that time. She baked a sweet cake and made polenta –
yellow grits that we ate hot with fried onions on top,
for lunch or dinner. Part of it was saved for the next
morning. Cold, it was cut into small squares that were
dunked into the hot coffee. During that time our diet
consisted mainly of beans and polenta. Still it must
have been a happy time for me as those two items
remain on my favorite-foods list. We were not

running or hiding. Life had resumed a certain routine. I had both parents with me. yet I was allowed a lot of freedom and I made new friends.

A little girl called Erica Bondi visited occasionally with her parents. Erica was five or six, so about a year or two younger than I was by then. Once, when the two of us played along the seawall, she fell into the shallow water below. She was not hurt, although soon after she developed an infection, details of which were not shared with me. I do remember being very concerned.

One evening Erica's father brought a freshly killed rabbit over to our house. My mother, who was an excellent cook, prepared it in some fancy way and the two families enjoyed a rare meal.

In Selce I went to school; I could read better than most of the children in the first grade since I had already been reading simple children's stories in Zagreb. One of my favorite books describes a city waking up in the early morning hours with illustrations of the baker delivering bread, the milkman milk, etc. The colors and the paper were a far cry from the beautiful books I read these days to my little granddaughters. It was not so easy with the writing. I had to practice those straight and curved lines of penmanship over and over again, under my father's vigilant eye. He wanted nothing but perfection. Maybe that is why, despite being a physician, I have reasonably legible handwriting.

One day I was walking to the dentist to have my first cavity filled, when a big boy from school started chasing me. He threw stones at me and called me

"Jew Girl". I ran as fast as I could. I tripped and fell.
I dried my bloody knee on the edge of my white
summer dress with red polka dots.
 You could hardly tell the blood from the dots.
Eventually he gave up the chase.

Selce was special in many ways. The tiny garden
in the back of the house had a big fig tree, which I
often climbed, settling on my favorite branch to read
and eat the luscious, sweet, just ripe, dark fruit. Trees
remained a conquerable challenge, even when fairly
high. If I was not in a climbing mood I could watch a
snail carry its house on its back across a fig leaf
that I placed in its path. Even today, despite the
wonderful garlicky aroma, you can't get me to eat
Escargot in even the best of French restaurants.

Above all, in Selce there was Bruno. His sister
Elvira was also there with her husband, Mr. Mandl,
who was older than her and had a teenage son, Ivo,
from a previous marriage. Elvira and my mother
became life-long friends. Mother was older, so Elvira
often came to her for advice, both then and years later.
Bruno and mother had worked for the same company
in Zagreb. Several years younger than my mother, he
was single. Before the war, one summer at the beach,
when I stepped on a live urchin, he had patiently taken
the sharp needles out of my foot, one by one, with
tweezers. In Selce we often walked along the shore
for what seemed like hours while Bruno told stories
about nature, such as the thousand-year-old fish

skeletons preserved in stone at the bottom of the ocean. Sometimes he would join me while I sat by the water with my line and hook waiting patiently for a little fish to get caught on the bait. Often Bruno caught a bigger fish and we would walk together back to the house where mother would fry them and serve them for dinner. Bruno was later caught and killed by the Ustase in a prison camp on one of the islands off the Dalmatian coast. This my parents found out from his sister Elvira who with her husband managed to join us safely in Taranto, in Southern Italy.

Then there were the trips to Crikvenica, a lovely seaside summer resort about two miles north of Selce. With the special permit from the Carabinieri, the Italian police, we left town for the day and walked the distance to go visit friends who were "in free confinement" in Crikvenica. The road was wide and straight, running along the seacoast, with villas on both sides. On the way we passed a house where two brothers, Roman and Ruben, lived. They were slightly older than I, both redheads. Used to spending time with boys, I considered myself lucky when I caught a glimpse of them playing on the front lawn behind the rosemary hedge that formed a fence for the property. The pungent odor of that herb which I use for my roast lamb often revives the memory of those days.

A little farther, directly facing the sea was a villa with another redhead, a teenager called Damir. It was his sister though who fascinated me. Her name was Tajana: a small girl with very dark short hair, she was about seven, I was almost eight by then.

We became the best of friends later in Italy. It was murmured that her family had tried to pass – pass for Gentile that is- by wearing crosses. There were Jews who hoped to save their life and that of their children's by professing to be Catholics.

One of the trips to Crikvenica remains documented by a photo in which I am sitting on the seawall wearing my best light blue dress with pleated bodice, salvaged from Zagreb. My mother, smiling, is standing next to me.

Mother and I

Penciled on the back of the picture in my dad's handwriting is the name of the place and the year 1942. Judging from the clothes we wore it must have been late spring or early fall. Selce was not to last forever.

Kraljevica

Having disposed of the remaining Jews in the German Zone of Yugoslavia by substituting organized killing in the Camps to the East for the random slaughter by the Ustase, in the summer of 1942 Hitler turned his attention with increasing persistence to the Croatian Jews who had found refuge in the Italian zone. A written communication from his Staff at the Foreign Ministry dated August 21st, 1942 informed Mussolini that the German and Croatian authorities wanted the Italian Military in the occupied territory to enact a plan to transfer the Croatian Jews to the East, leaving no doubt that this would lead to their elimination.

Mussolini signed the document with a "nulla osta" meaning there was no objection. The Second Italian Occupation Army under the Command of General Roatta decided to sabotage the decision. Delay tactics were devised including the need for a census, to be accomplished by moving the Jews to internment camps.

From that moment on, the efforts of the Italian Army to save us are well documented in official Italian-German correspondence. It should be noted that while Mussolini signed the order, Count

Ciano his Foreign Minister opposed handing over the Croatian Jews. In January 1944, the dying Fascist Regime of Mussolini executed Ciano as a traitor.

One day, in late fall 1942, we were told to pack because we were going to be relocated. Although I was a child, I realized that our future was uncertain, so I took with me a few lumps of sugar I had wrapped in colored paper and had saved for just such an event. All the Jews of Selce were rounded up and loaded onto trucks, to be taken to an unknown destination.

We were taken to a concentration camp near a town called Kraljevica. On arrival we were given photo identity cards; the date of entry into the camp,

handwritten, was November 1st, 1942.

The Identity Cards

Kraljevica means Kingstown, but there was nothing royal about the camp. Rows of long, wooden barracks were surrounded by a barbed wire fence. The men's barracks were in a separate area from those of the women. Girls and young boys stayed with their mothers and the older boys went with their fathers. Mother was very upset when they took her husband away from her. At first we did not know whether we would see father again.

Camp turned out to be a mixed blessing. It was a concentration camp to be sure. The barracks had no heat in winter. We slept on bunk beds, two to a bed. Mother and I were lucky to get the top berth, a small wooden ladder giving access to it. The food was scant and not very nourishing, especially for a growing youngster. We washed with cold water – when we did. I got scurvy on the back of my hands, which soon looked and felt like leather. Still, the Italians did not torture us, shoot us, or gas us. We were allowed to live.

A few days after our arrival the Jewish elders wrote a letter to the Camp Commandant thanking him for our safety.

Not everyone was able to adjust. The camp was built on terrain sloping down towards the seashore. Past the last barracks were the toilets, little cubicles that opened onto a narrow passage. It was in this passage that one morning a Jewish man was found hanging from the rafters. The news spread rapidly through the camp (before the war my parents would have shielded me from news of such an event); we children knew the spot where he was found and always pointed to it when we passed by. The image of the dead man, who had taken his own life, left a disturbing and lasting impression on my young mind.

Mornings started with a wake-up when they served chicory coffee from a large kettle. I had a deep voice for a small girl, and my first question when I woke up was: "Is coffee here yet?" This delighted the other kids who used to make fun by mimicking my voice and echoing my call. Everybody got a big ladle of the delicious black sweet liquid. Coffee that has chicory in it, still tastes like Camp as does a certain kind of minestrone, which was the most frequent daily meal. Once in a while you could find little bits of Parmesan cheese at the bottom of your bowl and that was a treat. Later the children were given a special nutritional supplement, consisting of a thick split pea soup which most of us disliked intensely and likened to loose excrements using a colorful term in the Croatian language. The women took turns sweeping the floor of the barracks. Some of them, I am sure, had never used a broom before.

A certain amount of social interaction took place between some internees and the Italian military. One officer fell in love with a young Jewish woman who became pregnant and delivered a little boy. They eventually got married and, since she and my mother remained very good friends for many years, I saw the child grow into a fine young man.

The Italian Commander in charge of the Camp allowed the Jewish men to organize a life for us that resembled some degree of normalcy. In one of the barracks in the men's section of the camp Friday night services were held. We used to get dressed as if it were still peacetime. I wore my blue velvet dress with the white lace collar. That was the time we got to see father and the other men. During the Jewish Holiday of Hanukkah we had a special festive dinner and a lottery. One of the prizes was a small doll's house that one of the camp inmates had built. I very much longed to own it, but we did not draw a winning number.

Once father got sick. He developed jaundice and was taken to the hospital in Kraljevica. Mother and I were allowed to leave the camp and visit him and I remember seeing him in his hospital bed. He had lost weight and had a yellowish complexion. Mother had baked meringues for him since he was on a strict diet and could eat very little. Where and how she got the eggs and sugar to bake them I still don't know, but they tasted delicious.

As for me I continued to climb trees in camp as I had done previously in Selce. Periodically someone would notify mother that Evica (my Croatian nickname) had been spotted up in the branches of a tall tree. My mother, trusting in my abilities, dismissed them with a brief, "I know; don't worry."

Once I did have a little mishap. I scraped my foot on the bark of a tree. First it was just a scratch but soon it became an abscess and I had to be taken to the Infirmary to have it lanced. I can still recall the icy feeling of the ethyl chloride the doctor used as a local anesthetic.

Then there was the time when I had tonsillitis, as almost every winter before and after, until they removed my tonsils years later. I lay on my bunk bed all day, feverish, wondering what would happen to me. Surely they could not take me to the University Hospital in Zagreb – the University where I thought I would go to medical school one day when the war was over. Even as a young child of four, asked what I would do as a grown up, I would readily respond: "I will be a doctor, have three children and a car." Zagreb's Medical School, on the *Salata* at the outskirts of the city, was well known for its excellence and often mentioned at home.

I was eight and a half years old now so I had to attend the camp school that the elders had organized; there were enough internees who could serve as teachers. I don't remember what I learned there, but I do remember being caught knitting one day, instead of paying attention to the teacher. I had to stay in class after school when my classmates went down to the edge of camp to bathe in the sea. On a nice summer day they actually marched a group of grown-ups and children to a real commercial beach with a pool. From the tall trampoline I jumped into the water, fearless and a bit of a show-off. To reach the beach we walked single file, escorted by the Italian soldiers, along a narrow path, through the woods and between the lovely shrubs of the Adriatic coastline.

During our stay in Kraljevica an attempt was made to send a group of children to Israel. A young man gathered us at the back of the camp, by stacks of lumber – leftovers from the building of barracks – and told us about the wonderful land of Israel, the old biblical home of the Jews, a place where all the people were Jewish, where Jews worked the earth and cultivated the soil. These stories made a great impression on me and to this day planks of wood stacked outdoors in a lumberyard bring this scene vividly back to my mind. Some of the children went, including my friend Ruth. My parents decided to keep me with them, although I am sure I would have gone if left to my own devices.

Rab, Armistice

In the meantime the war raged on.

In early 1943, dissatisfied with the Italian delay tactics, Ribbentrop, the German Foreign Minister went to Rome himself to discuss the matter with Mussolini in person. Mussolini officially consented to the transfer of the Croatian Jews to Trieste near the border between Italy and Yugoslavia, where the Germans would arrange for their deportation.

Soon after Ribbentrop left the room, his Excellency Robotti, Commandant of the Italian Second Army, who had been summoned to Rome and who was well aware of what fate awaited the Jews in German custody, convinced Mussolini that the handover of the Jews was against Italian interests, whereupon the Duce agreed to whatever delay tactics were necessary to prevent the handover.

We were transferred again, between May and June 1943, this time to another camp on the island of Rab (*Arbe* in Italian). In peacetime, the island was, and still is, a well-known resort. It was written up in the

NY Times Travel Section a few years ago and merits five pages in a recent Croatia travel guide. We had even spent one summer vacation there when I was a baby.

Rab camp was different in that there were small wooden barracks where families could stay together. We were reunited with father. The downside was that the camp was located in a marshy region full of mosquitoes. Many residents, including my mother, became infected with malaria, which later on almost cost all our lives. Here the latrines were distant from the barracks and there was a strong smell of disinfectant. I now realize it was chlorine. We had to walk a partly muddy path to reach the latrines, particularly unpleasant at night. As the adults tried to cope with the new reality, the children were left mostly unsupervised.

Again we were cared for reasonably well. But next to ours was a camp for Prisoners of War from Slovenia who were treated very badly by their captors. When the camp eventually dissolved, the Italian camp commander cut his veins rather than fall into the hands of the inmates sure to take revenge for their mistreatment.

In Rab I discovered modesty. It was summer. In an open area of the camp there was a large space surrounded by a canvas wall where women and children went to sun themselves in the nude. I resented the forced shared nudity then, as I would during showers later, when we were finally safe and were sent for delousing in large groups.

By now I was nine and I became more aware of our circumstances. Father told me stories about Stalin who from a simple peasant had risen to be the head of the Russian nation. He told me about people with red stars who were fighting Hitler. From an old red patent leather belt father cut out for me a small shiny red star like the ones (that I would discover later) adorned the caps of Tito's Partisans. During the war, the atrocities of the Stalinist era were not well known, but after the war when father had the opportunity to return to Yugoslavia, which was by then a Communist State run by Marshal Tito, he chose to remain in the West. Father never had any desire to go back, not even for a short visit, and when a well-known movie director who was shooting a film in Yugoslavia asked him to come along as interpreter and advisor, he refused the well-paying job.

In camp my father and other men had established contact with the mainland and the Partisans. (The Partisans, led by Tito, were those Yugoslavs who were against Fascism, against Hitler, and who fought their own war of liberation supported by the British.)

The war was not going well for the Italians. Mussolini was ousted in July 1943 and a new Italian government made a separate peace with the Allied Forces. The Armistice was signed on September 8, 1943.

Soon after the Armistice our Italian guards left. The camp doors were open. We were free! But free to go where? A group of us with our belongings hiked to the nearby woods until someone could find out if it was safe to go into town. It was known that the locals changed their loyalties according to the occupying forces. We camped in a small clearing surrounded by trees. One lady was a puppet maker and she entertained me with her puppets made of colorful fabric and wool. They were about nine or ten inches tall and had no strings. Amongst them was a queen with blond tresses in a long pale blue dress. There was a king and there were other characters but I liked the queen best and the woman gave her to me as a gift before we left those woods. Sadly I don't remember what happened to the queen with blond tresses. Visiting street fairs, to this day I am attracted to the puppet display, which brings me back to that time. It may have felt like a magical adventure to me, yet it was full of anxiety for my parents.

The next day we went down into the town of Rab. We were housed in a large hotel situated in a beautiful garden. The hotel was used as a makeshift hospital where we stayed because mother was suffering with recurrent high fevers and chills due to the malaria. Other occupants suffered from mental disorders, scarred by the horrors of the war.

From the front of the hotel, which was built on a hill overlooking the town, a long walk led down to the little port. In the back there were miles of fir-tree forests with narrow red clay paths that extended down to the seacoast. Soon I had a friend whose name was

Ivo. He and I would run along dirt paths, or just straight through the woods down to the water, with the speed of our nine year old legs, exploring the many wonders of nature. Mother spent most of the time in bed or at least in her hotel room. Father was often away, traveling to the mainland making contact with the Partisans and trying to arrange for our safe getaway.

I remember Rab as a beautiful island: I roamed the woods, I sat on the pier with my fishing pole, small worms for bait, or I jumped from rock to rock looking for shells and studying the little creatures that stuck tenaciously to the stone. I learned how to make bows and arrows out of thin pliable wooden sticks, as well as rudimentary kites that would actually fly. I used flour and water mixture as glue. Later in Rome when proper colored sheets of tissue paper and regular glue were available I was to improve considerably on my kite-making techniques.

In Rab father and I would visit a farm and buy milk and eggs: the warm raw milk that had just been squirted from the cow's udder into a metal bucket and which the farmer had poured out into a glass for me to drink, tasted delicious. At night, during a storm with thunder and lightening, I stood at the window of our room and watched the whole town and its old castle suddenly light up for a few seconds.

Other memories of Rab are less pleasant. Among the patients in the hotel were two mentally ill Albanians. One was young, in his twenties I would guess. He wore hospital clothes, all white, and went around talking about things no one understood, at times singing softly. He looked very disturbed. They said the Germans had massacred his family in front of his eyes.

The other man was older, somewhere between forty and fifty. He often dressed in women's clothes with high-heeled shoes, a pocketbook, and bright red lipstick. Or he might drape himself in a white bed sheet as a Roman citizen and paint his face white from the pit of spent lye on the hotel grounds. People would laugh at him and make fun of him. He could get very angry and strike out; as children we were both fascinated and scared of him.

But we were again in mortal danger. Having lost their Italian allies, the Germans were now coming down the Dalmatian coast taking over towns, villages, and islands formerly occupied by the Italians. Tito's Partisans were fighting fiercely to rid Yugoslavia both of the Ustase and the Germans but were no match for the power of the Wehrmacht.

One day a large ship docked in the port. It came to evacuate the Jewish refugees. While many boarded, we were unable to leave because mother was having a bout of high fever and was too ill to travel. In the days that followed I would often accompany my father and other Jewish men, who stood at the pier looking out across the sea for German boats that were bound to come sooner or later. I can only guess that a sense of dread and expectation went through my young mind at the time. I don't think I was aware that it was a death-watch.

Then one more boat came, a fishing trawler. There were wounded partisans on board who were being evacuated to southern Italy, by now in the hands of the Allied forces. There was room on board for another fifty to a hundred people. Each one of us was allowed only a limited amount of luggage. Mother, who by now had recovered from her fever, father and I went onto the ship; others did not. Some seemed frightened of the dangerous voyage, others were unwilling to relinquish their precious belongings.
These people missed their last chance. When the SS arrived, they slaughtered all the Jews left on Rab.

As night fell, the boat left. We started on a trip where I had many new experiences and visited strangely beautiful places. We only traveled by night, quietly, in complete darkness trying to avoid being spotted by the German ships cruising in the area. During the day, as we headed south, we anchored in small hidden bays off the beautiful and sometimes wild Dalmatian coastline. At night I would lie on a deck bench under the dark star-studded sky overhead and daydream. One night I was holding in my hand a tiny blue glass mug, a present from my favorite Aunt Zlata; it slipped from my grip and disappeared in the waves.

Aunt Zlata, Uncle Hinko and my cousin Ria, a teenager with thick, wavy chestnut hair of whom I was very fond (she was like an older sister to me,) were killed in Jasenovac in 1944. Uncle Hinko and mother had once been in love, but she belonged to the poor side of the family so his parents insisted he marry Aunt Zlata, mother's cousin, instead.

Of course I only found out about this later when mother showed me a ring Hinko had given her after serving in World War I. The ring was made of lead from a spent shell; it was lined in gold bearing the inscription "to Olga" and the date. One of the reasons I was so fond of Aunt Zlata was that when I visited her in Zagreb she let me help her bake in her big kitchen. Her grandmother, who was also my mother's grandmother, was living with them at the time. A big, old lady dressed in black, she sat in a large chair and had many brown age-spots on her hands. When I look at the spots that now appear on the back of my own hands, I think with tenderness about the older lady and aunt Zlata's home.

Now, on the boat that was taking us south, I was not allowed to go downstairs where the wounded lay. But one night we had to stay in port because German ships had been sighted in the area. The Partisans came on shore with us, built a fire with sticks, and we all sat around it listening to their heroic battle stories. And I learned to twirl a branch with an incandescent tip very fast in the air and watch the glowing designs it made against the black sky.

During the day my father left port with a fellow traveler and took me along for a walk. The path that led to the top of the village was flanked by private homes surrounded by walled-in gardens. For the first time I saw orange trees rich with their fruit extending above the walls. During that walk, another first, I heard my father use a curse word while talking with the other man. Yes, I had learned those words from other children in camp, but somehow I never expected to hear one uttered by my father. Imperceptibly, I was growing up.

Vis – the Americans – Tuturano – Taranto – Rome

Eventually we were able to leave and proceed with our voyage south. After a few days we reached Vis, an island located out in the Adriatic Sea between the Dalmatian Coast and Italy, occupied in 1943 by the Americans. After the war it became a Yugoslav Naval Base and was off-limits to tourists for many years. On our arrival and as we got off the boat, father was carrying our two suitcases, which had somehow survived our travails, while mother was holding me by the hand. We were greeted by an air-raid alarm as German planes were strafing the island. While running for cover off the road, father ripped his raincoat on the valise.

He was angry, blamed mother over the torn coat. It hardly made sense now that we were almost safe. Nerves must have been frayed. Still, as always when they argued, it was very upsetting to me. The green field nearby, studded with white narcissus, was a paradox with the menacing sound of the sirens and the grown-ups arguing.

We were directed to a large school – yes, a school again – blankets were placed on the floor and each of us staked out the territory where we would sleep and which would be our home for the time being. The Americans gave us canned corned beef and condensed milk, little red cans with carnations on them. It was real food but also novel. Condensed milk still tastes like Vis and no one in my family believes me when I say Spam tasted delicious. In my hospital cafeteria, when available, I frequently chose corned beef hash for lunch, the closest thing to the Spam of my memory.

During the day I explored the garden and the orchard behind the school. Almond trees were in bloom and I made a friend, a young American soldier. I don't know how we communicated, but we did. Perhaps Tante Rosenberg's teaching had left me with enough knowledge of English to get by. It was my first grown-up friend since Bruno. The friendship came to an end quickly when we left Vis on a big transatlantic ship operated by the British Navy. It was taking the wounded partisans, and us, to safety in southern Italy.

It was a bumpy voyage on rough seas. Everyone became ill. Nevertheless I made friends with the captain. He took me into the control cabin and then offered me hot porridge to eat from a big enamel bowl that looked like a chamber pot. I seem to remember saying something like: "Thank you, but no thank you," as that kind of hot cereal was not something one ate in my part of the world, especially not from a chamber pot.

When the ship anchored off the southern Adriatic coast of Italy we were taken to a small place called Tuturano, near the town of Brindisi. It had previously been a POW camp for British soldiers captured by the Italians during the African campaign in Libya. We were in a camp again, and it would not be the last. We were taken to showers to get clean. (Happily we did not know then – or at least I did not – that the Germans herded the Jews, naked, to presumed showers where, when the doors were hermetically closed, the shower heads in the ceiling spewed the deathly Zyklon B which killed all inside.) Our clothes were disinfected, we were fed cheese and special crackers, the kind you can get in New York in Spanish *bodegas* and that the Italians called *gallette*, and then we waited.

I am not sure how long we stayed there, but for sure at least one night, as I remember a group of women sitting in the evening on the floor of the barracks, in a circle, while one of them was foretelling the future from a deck of cards. It was like a scene from the opera Carmen, where Carmen is in the mountains with her fellow smugglers; she reads her own future and keeps pulling the Queen of Spades while she sings "la mort, toujours la mort".

From Tuturano they moved us by truck to Taranto, the port city in the instep of Italy's boot in the region of Apulia. There we were placed in a refugee camp on the outskirts of town; it had low, salmon-colored stucco buildings with flat roofs. Most of Italy's buildings had flat roofs, quite a change from the gabled tiled roofs of my native Yugoslavia.

We did not stay in that camp very long. Father heard rumors that the Allies were planning to resettle the Jewish refugees in a new homeland in Africa. A thoroughly European man, my father would have none of it; he took mother and me on a trip into town and we never went back to the camp. We were to stay in Taranto for a year and a half, until the end of the war. With some of the money that we had been able to take out of Zagreb, my parents rented an apartment on the 2nd floor of a two-story walk-up, from a woman whose husband was a Prisoner of War in Russia. She lived across the hall and sang all day, always the same two tunes: The song "Amapola" and another one, whose first few verses "Vola colomba bianca vola, dimmelo tu che tornera" translate, "Fly my white dove, fly, tell me he will return." At first I did not know what all the words meant, but I was to learn soon enough.

I recall my parent's bedroom best. It was decorated in cream-colored furniture with large mirrors. I would now call it Art Deco. The Allied Forces who occupied Taranto considered us friendly war refugees so we were given special privileges. Among other things, we were allowed into theaters that showed American movies and we received clothes and food from the UNRRA (United Nations Relief and Rehabilitation Administration).

I remember a short-sleeve, brown jersey dress with elastic bodice, which I wore but disliked, and big chunks of American cheddar cheese, which I liked very much. The UNRRA also established schools for the refugees where mother learned to sew. This came in very handy, as for many years, while father was struggling to make a living, she was able to sew all my summer dresses.

Among the Yugoslav refugees in Taranto was a couple, good friends of my parents: Fee and Zigec Singer. They could not have children because the SS had rendered Fee, a German Jew, sterile. This couple loved me as if I had been their own daughter and the love was mutual. I was very fond of Zigec who bought me my first real doll since Zagreb, a little baby boy I named Mitzco. I adored Fee. She was about ten years younger than mother, which means she was then in her mid-thirties. She was good looking in a flamboyant way. Tall, slim with long wavy chestnut hair and a large mouth, full lips emphasized by red lipstick. She liked men and they liked her and Zigec did not seem to mind.

We often received items from the U.S. Navy supply stores for which we had Fee Singer to thank since she was very friendly with the Occupation troops and always had cigarettes to spare. Mercifully neither my mother nor my father smoked, but I benefited from Fee's heavy cigarette habit in that I got the empty boxes of Lucky Strike, Kit Cat and others, which could be made into belts and other useful objects.

I was then able to fulfill my dream of having a dollhouse by building one myself. For example, I made a chest of drawers by stacking empty matchboxes with glue and making little knobs to pull the drawers out. It was with mother and Fee that I got to see my first Betty Grable and Esther Williams films.

Fee and Zigec, like many of us, went to Rome after the war. They soon left for the US when their immigration Quota came due. The Singers made a new home in an apartment in Forest Hills, Queens. It was Fee who, when I came to Brooklyn as a young bride, took me to Manhattan and introduced me to Bloomingdale's where she bought me a black winter coat with a little fur collar.

During the war the Allied Navy was anchored in the port of Taranto and large deterrent helium balloons were seen in the sky offshore. In summer when we went swimming our feet and especially my smart, one-piece white bathing suit were often stained with heavy black machine oil, which was pretty hard to remove.

A drawbridge separated old and new Taranto. Every day at a fixed time, in the afternoon, the drawbridge opened to let the ships of the Allied Navy through into the inner harbor. More often than not that time would find father and me near the bridge watching the aircraft carriers, and the warships go through. Sometimes father and I would cross the bridge into the old city. We walked the narrow lanes, where laundry hung from window to window and tiny shops nestled in the old buildings that had been there from time immemorial. Father might go into a shop and bargain for a needed item. Children of all ages played in the street and adults sat on chairs placed on the sidewalk so that the street became an extension of their homes.

In Taranto I again became friends with Tajana. She was the girl who lived in the house by the sea on the road from Selce to Crikvenica and wore the big cross. There was no need now to disguise being Jewish. By now we were almost ten years old; we became inseparable. We climbed dirt hills near the beach pretending they were enemy fortresses and we played a crazy game we called "granny's game." The game consisted of ringing someone's doorbell then running away. If someone should open the door before our safe escape we asked if grandma was home. We also pretended to have a magic wand with which we could make objects disappear and then reappear again. My parents always thought that was very funny. A year or so later in Rome we would spit cherry pits on passersby from Tajana's 10th floor balcony. I wonder now who the mastermind behind those pranks was.

In the Art Deco bedroom in Taranto I had one of the scariest experiences of my life. I was ill with a high fever, lying in my parents' double bed when I suddenly sat up unable to breathe. It was especially scary because I could see myself in a large mirror across from the bed. I don't know how many seconds went by before I could breathe again. My parents' explanation was that I was given too large a dose of quinine to treat an attack of presumed malaria contracted in the mosquito-infected camp of Rab.

One day that summer I developed a severe case of whopping cough. I had to spend nights in a rocking chair on a small balcony facing the courtyard to get some cooler air. To help me recover and escape the stifling heat the doctor recommended taking me out of the city for a few days. My parents rented a room in a small *pensione* in the town of Martina Franca in the countryside outside Taranto. From the first floor window of our bedroom, facing a main road, I saw motorcycle races for the first time. The center of town consists entirely of white conical stone buildings called *Trulli,* which are typical for that region. They were very different from city apartment buildings or village homes I had seen anywhere else. The size of a small cottage with one large room, two at most, with a carefully tended flower garden in front, they could have been created by a child's imagination.

Back in Taranto, the occupied city, soldiers were everywhere. The Military Police with their short clubs were ready to return order when necessary. Some houses had an *Out of Bounds* sign prominently displayed. When I inquired about it I was told it meant soldiers were not allowed to go there. It took some years before I realized those were houses of prostitution. Soldiers frequently got drunk and one night when we came home we found one sprawled on the threshold of our apartment, blocking our entrance. Father had to call the Military Police; two of them came and carried the soldier away.

In the meantime the money hidden in the teddy bear and in mother's girdle started to run out. Father was faced with the need to provide for his family. Seeing that there was a demand for hard liquor, he and a friend opened a liquor company that did its own bottling. I am not sure how successful they were in their enterprise but I still have one or two labels with the words Silver Star written in silver on a green background.

Across the street from our apartment house was a garage where American soldiers repaired their jeeps and painted their trucks. I hung around at the garage.

I liked the smell of gasoline and turpentine, still do. The soldiers gave me small cans filled with bright red and yellow paint, which found its way onto miniature clay vases and pots, local craft, that my parents had bought for me. My mother saved a plain, glazed 10-inch pitcher from that time. When she died it passed on to me and, even if somewhat chipped, it remains one my treasured possessions.

The Allied Forces in Taranto comprised British troops, American troops, and also the Jewish brigade, young men living in Palestine who had volunteered to fight the Germans alongside the British. These young soldiers assembled the Jewish refugee children and taught us about Israel, about life in the Kibbutz and the Hebrew language – today I can still speak a few short sentences.

There was also a Swiss soldier who was part of the Coast Guard and who took me for a ride in the harbor on his motorboat. The speed and the water splashing all over me were exhilarating. Being away from his own family he enjoyed having found an adoptive one in Taranto. Once he joined us and other friends on an outing to a nearby beach. Someone took a photo of all of us standing on the white sand in front of a group of pine trees.

Since we now lived in Italy I had to learn the language well enough to attend school. In July 1944, I turned ten years old. First I was sent for private lessons to a kindly middle-aged spinster. I walked to her apartment alone and there she taught me Italian grammar and vocabulary, but also kept giving me little cardboard pictures of the Madonna, Baby Jesus, and the Saints. I recall liking the Madonna, always beautiful and dressed in a long blue cloak. I am not sure how these images were handled by my parents and what eventually happened to them.

On one of my trips home from my class I got into trouble. I passed a Church and saw that a wedding was in progress. I remembered that mother had once mentioned casually that they had beautiful weddings in the churches and that I might enjoy seeing one some day. (Mother knew about Christian weddings because she grew up in an integrated community in Hungary.) So I went in, sat in a pew and watched. Mesmerized by the ceremony I stayed... and stayed, while my parents went crazy looking for me. I never forgot the look of anguish on their faces when I finally showed up, a look which soon turned to anger. I made it a point from then on not to be late again. Even years later when I went to parties with my friends I called my parents if my return home was delayed.

After my Italian language improved I was sent to a regular school run by nuns. The school was in a large building with a courtyard where palm trees grew. There we had to march in formation – "Right face, left face, forward march!" – despite the fact that Italy had surrendered and Fascism had fallen. The problem was that I have right-left disorientation. So I was always out of step and embarrassed. Still, I enjoyed school, especially the ancient history that focused on the myths of the founding of Rome and the history of the early kingdoms that followed.

Finally, one day, the war did end. People by the hundreds were in the streets rejoicing. Soon we were to move north to Rome where dad thought he would have better opportunities to make a living. The prospect of the move overjoyed me; now I would see the city where all that history I had studied about took place. Travel was still a challenge; we had to take a bus to the Adriatic port city of Bari and from Bari another bus to Rome. The trip took us north through bombed-out towns, the walls of buildings crumbling, inner rooms exposed and full of bullet holes. The most damaged of these was Salerno where a major battle had taken place between the Allied forces and the Germans.

We entered Rome through the Porta San Paolo, an opening in the wall that surrounds the city. The wall was built in the third century A.D. Next to the opening, a white stone pyramid, a funerary chamber for a Roman Tribune of the first century B.C. was the first landmark I saw. I was awestruck. There, at the end of the war, eleven years old, I started a new life and a love affair with a city - a love affair that continues even after many years of separation. I was to stay in Rome until age 26 when, with my newborn son and a medical degree, I joined my husband in my new home: New York City, USA.

Acknowledgements

I learned in detail about the efforts of the Italian Army through *All or Nothing: The Axis and the Holocaust 1941-1943,* by Jonathan Steinberg, which my daughter Irene sent to me in the early Nineties. Quite recently Francoise and Ned Marcus made available to me a monograph published in 1945 by Leon Poliakov and Jacques Sabille, *Jews under Italian Occupation,* New York 1991, an invaluable reference which helped substantiate many of my memories and put a more exact time frame on the sequence of events.

Other sources I consulted to furnish the reader with a minimal historical background are: John R. Lampe, *Yugoslavia as History*, Cambridge University Press

1999; Martin Gilbert, *The Second World War,* revised edition, Henry Holt and Company, New York 1991. Some of these events are covered in a Video produced by The National Center for Jewish Film: *The Righteous Enemy.*

This manuscript could not have been completed without the repeated reading and
patient editing by my daughter Irene Appelbaum of Missoula, Montana. My thanks also, to Marlene Roberts of Highland Beach, Florida, for her suggestions and editing and to Edmund Byrne of Ardsley, New York who read my manuscript and helped me with the final needed changes.